Burn Down the American Plantation:

Call for a Revolutionary Abolitionist Movement

Burn Down the American Plantation:
Call for a Revolutionary Abolitionist Movement

Published in the United States by comrades of the
Revolutionary Abolitionist Movement

http://revolutionaryabolition.org

This book was written and published to inspire a new generation of
revolutionaries.

Table of Contents

Introduction

As revolutionary dreams evaporated, the century turned, and poverty and despair became etched so deeply into our existence that the lofty political dreams we aspired to in the past became myths. The Black Panther Party and Black Liberation Army's actions have become distant legend, and their political stances tales. Nixon's counter-revolution transitioned smoothly to Reagan's and then to Clinton's, with such sheer barbarism the cities still have yet to clean their bloodstained streets. As family after family was torn apart and poverty took its toll, our revolutionary history wasn't denied, but simply forgotten. Even as the fighters of the recent past sit behind penitentiary walls and the symbols of revolution were transformed into commodities, their revolutionary intentions were buried, and forgotten by many.

With the rise of 20th Century liberation movements in the United States and abroad—from socialist and national liberation struggles to the Black Panther Party—the US government fought to ensure its hegemonic dominance of the world system. The powerful proclaimed the "End of History," the black revolution had been overwhelmed, and socialist movements discredited due to the Soviet Union's centralization and collapse. The US-led capitalist world system finally had complete hegemonic reign over the entire globe. George Bush proclaimed a "New World Order" and Bill Clinton had the liberty to act freely on the world with little impediment to US power. Despite this, unforeseen cracks quickly emerged.

The world of the powerful, which appeared so secure, was rapidly disintegrating into a hellish nightmare of endless war, bloodshed, and permanent strife. Yet the limits of the United States' power has become clear. In recent years, the US spent massive amounts of money on military to buttress its political ineptness. This strategy was a remarkable failure as its military weakness became apparent with colossal failures in Iraq, Palestine, and the Americas.

The US government continuously played a sordid double game on its population, preaching sermons of peace while delivering war, extolling the virtues of success while providing destitution, singing the songs of freedom while creating the largest prison society on earth. The government has diligently rendered the society so bereft and fatigued that many simply found it easier to ignore the slavery and despotism outside their own door. Our collective imaginations have become so impoverished that many have trouble even dreaming of a better world.

This was not the case everywhere. In Chiapas, Mexico armed rebels emerged from the jungle fighting for dignity, bearing an anti-state egalitarian ideology reminiscent of the Spanish revolution. Masked fighters began besieging summit meetings in capital cities across the globe. Revolutionaries formed an autonomous enclave in Athens, Greece, and armed groups launched a war against their government. Uprisings and social movements continued to arise, with eloquent defiance, trying to chart a new path for revolutionary momentum around the globe; they each outlined new possibilities and pitfalls, but also illuminated the scope of our historic problems. In the United States, new movements arose, but few grounded themselves firmly enough to pass the strategic threshold necessary for revolutionary change. As they ebb and flow, the misery of American society has become increasingly entrenched. The need for organization beyond protest movements is glaringly obvious.

What we find the need to articulate here is that the political situation in the US—while increasingly violent and volatile, and rapidly developing — is a clear continuation of the policies that have been enacted since the Civil War. Essentially, the Civil War never ended. The struggle against chattel slavery, from neighborhoods demolished by the 'war on drugs' to the prison-industrial apparatus, and resistance to US expansion across the continent is the same war being waged today in another form. The primary question, then, is how do we organize to abolish slavery, and stop the expansion of the slave-project?

The State, in complicity with white supremacist organizations, has done everything in its capacity to ensure that the relations of slavery were entrenched in US political, social, and economic life. In doing so it ensured that its slave populace, and other targeted populations, would remain in bondage, trapped in its carceral apparatuses. In reaction to the rise of the Black Lives Matter movement and the rise of a black man to the height of its political machine, coupled with the decline of US imperial power in the 21st Century, hegemonic power birthed the only logical solution to preserving its dominant grip: a fascist movement to take control of the State. The ascendance of Donald Trump to power is the natural outcome of the white supremacist state.

It is in this context that a revolutionary political movement must reawaken. We cannot just rely on the movements of the recent past. We must look at the beginning of the struggle against slavery to properly orient our actions, while also adapting models from the successful revolutionary projects of our own time.

History will judge the decisions we make today, and the targets of our ire have never more clear. Will we standby and watch as the State continues to confine millions in its detention camps? Will we allow another Mike Brown or Akai Gurley to be murdered in cold blood? Will we permit the ethnic cleansing of thirteen million people through industrial-scale deportation? As Mumia Abu Jamal exclaimed about Tamir Rice, "When a child dies, adults don't deserve to breathe their stolen air." Will we deserve to breathe while knowing that millions of people are still enslaved in our midst? Our historical mission is clear. We must burn down the American plantation once and for all.

The Black Struggle

The black position, with its struggle between overwhelming violence and the ceaseless drive for liberation, has always been the locus for any truly liberatory project in the United States must begin. The desire to escape bondage, to rid oneself of the totalizing violence that is black life in America, has proven to be impossible since, as instituted in law, and in deed, black life is trapped in the captivity of black skin itself. Through the actions of the State and society at large, we see time and time again that bondage and dehumanization have been etched into black existence, and like an apparition haunting the States, the black struggle has the potential to unleash the all-encompassing violence that is black life back onto the entire country until the racial question is truly rectified.

The difficulty in finding a political or social resolution is due to the fact that the system of slavery has not been abolished. It is still enshrined in legislation, and, more importantly, is codified into the subconscious makeup of the US citizenry. The plantation system in the American South no longer exists in its earlier historical form. The wage system of the North clearly established its hegemonic position over its competitor after the Civil War. However, the fundamental issue the abolitionists raised—the matter of slavery and slave society—was not only never resolved, but has been normalized, legitimized, and expanded. We see that the most egregious institutions of the 18th century are replicated in the 21st century in remarkably similar forms with similar effects.

In the 18th century people were transported across the Atlantic Ocean, hoarded beneath the bowels of squalid slave ships. Displayed on auction blocks like a miscellaneous object, people were marked, renamed, and separated from peers and loved ones to toil on southern plantations until they collapsed from stress, overwork, and misery. Today, the ships are simply correctional buses, the auction blocks are now the courtrooms, and people are indelibly marked with prison numbers that remain etched on their records till they die. Once institutionalized people internalize the deferment necessary to survive into a daily routine, this inevitably becomes a recreation of plantation life. Criminality, in the US, is then marked with the same coding as slave captivity, such that, in essence, blackness is enveloped with both distinctions. Whereas, whiteness, in contrast, is marked with what is deemed virtuous and the enforcement of these values. So, slavery and criminality are wedded as one and the same, and the reign of white supremacist terror and bondage becomes the imperative signifier.

The first obstacle to addressing slavery in the US is the misconception that relates slavery with a specific labor code, rather than a system, a lineage, and a stratified code of bondage, dehumanization and captivity. The slave system unquestionably included coerced, free labor, but looking at only the labor arrangements leads people to mistakenly assume that with the eradication of the labor code slavery was also eradicated. If we properly state, then, that slavery was not abolished in the US Civil War, we can redirect our understanding of the 19th century Abolitionist movement and recognize that the goal was not really achieved and the struggle continues today.

The establishment of the Atlantic world, and the modern world system overall, was constructed through the birth of the slave trade. The 16th century marks the beginning of the slave trade, the collapse of feudal system in England, and the beginning of the centralization of state power in England. This period marks the birth of capitalism, and ties capitalism's emergence with the devastation of the African continent, the slave system, and the genocide in the Americas. Thus, the spread of wage labor and capital in Europe and the Americas developed concurrently with slave labor, demarcation of border, centralization of state power and the creation of race.

Most of the terms we use today to understand the world arise from this period: African, European, black, white, America, capitalism, etc, all have their root in the growth of the current world system founded on white supremacy. As black liberation theorist Frank Wilderson notes:

The theoretical importance of emphasizing this in the early twenty-first century is twofold. First, capital was kick-started by approaching a particular body (a black body) with direct relations of force, not by approaching a white body with variable capital. Thus, one could say that slavery is closer to capital's primal desire than is exploitation. It is a relation of terror as opposed to a relation of hegemony. Second, today, late capital is imposing a renaissance of this original desire, the direct relation of force, the despotism of the unwaged relation. This renaissance of slavery—that is, the reconfiguration of the prison-industrial complex—has once again as it's structuring metaphor and primary target the black body.[1]

The "relation of terror" became the norm in the US, with genocidal incursions into Native American territory, and draconian slave patrols mercilessly constituting the new racial hierarchy. The majority of Native American nations were vanquished, US territory expanded from coast to coast, and blackness became indelibly inscribed with the mark of the slave. The US elite, cloaked with a language of liberty and freedom, established a political system, overtly, shamelessly, for the wealthy and powerful—as John Jay stated, "those who own the country ought to govern it."

Owning the country, by birthright, became a given for the propertied white population. Breeding part of the population like cattle was also a liberty that was forcefully enshrined in American practice. While the State marched shamelessly across the plains, and ventured into Latin America, the white establishment seized control over the bodies of all those in its path, encroaching upon the most intimate aspects their of humanity, rendering their incorporation into larger society practically impossible. The potential for human recognition vanished, and the far reaching nature of white supremacy became global as Native Americans were exterminated, and black people became enveloped in the slave-relation.

This was met with fierce resistance. From the Maroon fighters in the swamplands, to Nat Turner's armed rebellion; from Fredrick Douglass's cogent prose to the provocative story telling of Harriet Beecher Stowe, resistance to the system was constant. Maroon communities provided an example not only of resistance, but also of a social organization in the US that could escape the grasp of white supremacy. The Maroon societies existed from the self-declared "Revolutionary War" until the Civil War, as a loose-knit constellation of multi-racial group formations, that were fortified militarily and acted as a staging ground for guerrilla actions. They provided a network of support for those fleeing captivity and evading capture by the State. For instance, it seems that Nat Turner was attempting to reach their territory before being overwhelmed by reactionary militias. It is under these conditions that the Abolitionist movement was born, highlighted by John Brown's assault of Harper's Ferry and Harriet Tubman's armed, underground railroad.

Just as we live with the myth that the Civil Rights movement ended second-class citizenship, we have the myth that the Emancipation Proclamation ended slavery. In actuality it was a northern military strategy to break the southern planter class. Just as militant struggle is erased today, the autonomous action of black rebels, is ignored, and Lincoln is applauded for freeing people he never intended to free, didn't want to free, and in actuality didn't free. The US signed and ratified the 13th amendment, which abolished slavery, except as punishment for a crime. This exception rendered the entire notion of abolition false, and tragically succeeded in containing the larger freedom struggle in the US for some time.

In the immediate aftermath of the war, during the Reconstruction period, the black community established one of the most radical social experiments this country has ever seen. Erased by repression and social amnesia, it is not an overstatement for Angela Davis to call it, "one of the most hidden eras of US history." The black community instituted forward-looking non-commodified education system, socialized medical services, and progressive legislation challenging statutory white supremacy. As a result, even poor whites began benefiting from these programs.

In conjunction with the Southern planter class and in collusion with the Northern establishment, the White House scrambled to do whatever it could in order to reinstitute the same policies that gave slavery its foundational core. President Andrew Johnson, who came to office after Lincoln's assassination, has been often described as one of the most racist presidents in US history. Instead of supporting the community initiatives that would have eased racial antagonism, he enthusiastically supported the draconian black codes which restricted freedom of movement for black people, and trapped them in a labor economy based on share-cropping debt. Johnson vetoed legislation that would have given blacks land—while granting former plantations back to slave owners. He vetoed the Civil Rights bill and instead chose to support the rising white supremacist militia movements.

It was under this reign of racial terror that the US established itself as an industrial world power, with paramilitary KKK units forming in the South, increasingly cruel criminalization of black people in the North, and imperialist military ventures in far reaching areas of the globe, slaughtering and subjecting people from Haiti to the Philippines.

Meanwhile, revolutionary groups around the world began organizing concerted resistance against the world order. Militants around the world began espousing, and promoting self-organization against the international system for a different form of abolition—the abolition of the State and capitalism. Permeating in debate halls in France, cities in Russia, and small farms in Spain, a new revolutionary paradigm emerged that slowly started to penetrate into US political activity. When WEB DuBois portrayed slaves' refusal to work during the Civil War as a General Strike against the ruling classes, it marked a substantial departure in the theoretical underpinning of the resistance, and brought this struggle to the attention of revolutionaries worldwide to the war for liberation in the States. Around the globe there were massive shifts in the balance of power: the Czar fell in Russia, Mexico went headfirst into revolution, while militants in Spain, France, Italy, and China began to experiment and implement council and commune-based forms of revolutionary activity with goal of eradicating capitalism and the State. Militants in the US took notice of these movements and began applying their strategies and tactics to form their own liberation struggles at home. With rising fear of this influence, the US government launched the Red Scare, and a severe wave of repression culminating in raids, strike breaking, large swaths of deportations, and huge anti-black race riots.

While revolutionary fervor spread globally, the nation-state system became solidified and capitalism spread to every corner of the globe as imperialist states forced open markets that did not previously exist. This further forced arbitrary borders and European State institutions on people in every continent. World Wars—or preparation for them—became the norm. Militarization became a criterion for the stability of power, and authoritarian social organization seemingly became a practical necessity for survival, even for revolutionary movements. The armed partisans during the Spanish Revolution provided the only formidable alternative; expropriating vast landholdings from the wealthy, establishing workplace collectives and communes, arming feminist militias, and coming as close as any movement towards organizing a stateless society in an industrialized setting.

The rise of fascism coincided with the defeat of the Spanish Revolution, culminating in World War II. Europe had already wreaked incomprehensible devastation on much of the world. The same ceaseless drive for mechanization, centralized power, and racial purity solidified their legacy with the Holocaust, leaving the world in awe as the cruelty it practiced around the world turned in on itself in the most savage fashion imaginable.

In the United States, the 20th century also provided no reprieve from white supremacist violence; in actuality the modern plantation system further entrenched itself into the substratum of the American psyche. The attempt to recreate a new world, to build a better future, and escape the shackles of chattel slavery, proved impossible for black people as American society, true to form, established new modes of racial terror, and proclaimed the birth of a nation anointed by the noose. Black people fled to the North in the early 20th century and were met with new forms of criminalization in every city. From the Rosewood Massacre, to the Red Summer violence around the country, to the spreading of syphilis in the Tuskegee experiments, the terror continued unabated. As people died with dignity in the war for abolition, new generations of fighters arose, particularly inspired by the internationalist and anti-colonial struggles of the day.

Malcolm X set the new paradigm for resistance, launching a huge recruitment drive, training militants in self-defense, and preaching a philosophy of armed resistance "by any means necessary." Robert F. Williams' branch of the NAACP began arming and training its members, leading to several armed conflicts with the KKK. The Deacons for Defense, in Alabama and Mississippi, followed suit. But, it was the Black Panther Party for Self-Defense (BPP), that combined internationalism, armed self-defense, community programs and a solid political vision in such an intelligible, and inspiring manner that they became, and remain a model for revolutionary movements in the world today.

The BPP organized survival programs for the black population: breakfast programs, education, health services, transportation, while their newspapers and armed self-defense became vehicles for revolutionary momentum. The BPP encouraged other revolutionary groups to organize in their local communities, in a similar political fashion, and work in larger coalitions for freedom of oppressed groups. Their resistance inspired the growth of the American Indian Movement, the Young Lords, the Weather Underground, and other militant organizations that were working towards abolition and a communal life. The BPP organized armed patrols against police brutality which propelled them into popular consciousness and made their membership skyrocket. These patrols resulted in several armed conflicts with the police. The federal government declared them the most dangerous group in the country. The resulting repression drained the Panthers resources and, eventually, eradicated the groups growth. But the armed attacks from the State also led to the growth of the Black Liberation Army (BLA), the organization most feared by government in recent US history.

After the BPP suffered frequent and unanswered casualties, the guerrilla organization was established. The BLA was a clandestine organization, that attacked police, prisons, and banks, in a valiant attempt to drag the United States government into a guerrilla war on its own soil. BLA guerrilla, Assata Shakur notes, "…the Black Liberation Army was not a centralized, organized group with a common leadership and chain of command. Instead there were various organizations and collectives working together and simultaneously independent of each other."[2] The organization survived until the 1980's, well after the fervor of the 1960's rebellions subsided. Former BLA soldier, Russell Maroon Shoatz argued the BLA were "the most effective Black assault units since the maroons!"[3]

The Black Panther Party, while successful in many ways, was plagued by the same pitfalls that hindered other revolutionary groups around the world in the 20th century. The organization had a firm and unquestionable, leadership structure which was easily detained, discredited, and then destroyed. Furthermore, with all power lying in the hands of specific individuals, wider autonomy and fluidity was hindered. Equally as important, the BPP, had a militant stance but it did not have a larger militant strategy. When confronted with massive state violence the organization was forced on a defensive footing for the rest of its existence. It did not prepare for war until the war had begun. By the time of the BLA's creation the war had already entered a new phase, and the political bodies (the BPP) were now hardly functional, or were not giving cues to the guerrilla units. If these two organizations had functioned simultaneously and concertedly the current political situation would be very different in the US today.

In response to the black freedom struggle, the government meted out some of the cruelest prison sentences that the world had ever seen, while Reagan launched a war on drugs, which was really a euphemistic phrase for a war on black people and the urban working-class. Reagan's counter-revolution gutted social programs, criminalized Latino immigration, stigmatized Muslims, and ravaged the black community, creating an influx of drugs and growing poverty nationwide. As the Soviet Union collapsed the revolutionary aspirations of many around the world followed.

In the midst of the establishment of the uni-polar world order, under the banner of the New World Order, the United States ushered in a new period of free trade, attempting to liberalize markets all to further their political and economic sway around the globe. The US arranged an agreement with Mexico and Canada called the North American Free Trade Agreement (NAFTA), which opened North America's borders to capital flight, while at the same time restricting labor laws.

As the law went into effect, rebels in Mexico, inspired by Emiliano Zapata's guerrilla struggle, emerged from the Southeast, calling the economic agreement a "death sentence," for the indigenous and declaring war on the State. These new guerrillas eschewed the revolutionary paradigms of the 20th century and refused to vie for State power. Vehemently anti-capitalist and pro-feminist, the Zapatistas made alliances with revolutionary groups abroad and established a new revolutionary current, combining the thought of the Spanish revolution with local traditions. Inspired by the Zapatistas, rebels around the world began espousing anti-state thought, and besieged the meetings and conferences of the global elite. New connections were born, but these movements never developed the capacity to overthrow national governments. Rather they promoted ideas and actions that resonated across the world and demonstrated how anti-authoritarian decision-making could function.

The US, still firmly entrenched atop the world order, was already beginning to lose its political hegemony. It continued its endless wars in the Middle East, and stubbornly refused to distribute resources amongst its population. Wealth was being concentrated in fewer, and fewer hands, while the larger population was becoming increasingly destitute. Protest movements continued on the left and also developed on the right, each denouncing the corrupt political class, but for radically different reasons.

The Battle of Seattle in 1999, and subsequent clashes led to the growth of a larger movement committed to anarchist and anti-state principles. It is at this point that participation exploded in the revolutionary organizations of the modern period: the US Anarchist Black Cross Federations, the Earth Liberation Front, anti-fascist/anti-racist organization and an assortment of various of social centers and publications. These insurrectionary groups formed the militant backbone of the resistance in the United States. There is an impressive breadth of knowledge and activity from this period. While maintaining a network of public social centers and releasing dozens of influential texts, these groups also managed to develop resistance to wars, trade deals, and police violence, while also engaging in a diverse array of solidarity actions, ranging from prisoner letter writing campaigns, labor support, militant anti-racist resistance, and general attacks against the infrastructure of the State and capitalist institutions.

These newer resistance groups had varying degrees of success but their major limitation is that their traditions are rooted in the protest movements of the late 1990's rather than from insurgent movements of the 1970's or the larger abolitionist currents of the 19th century. A problem with historical memory arises, and the newer militants did not learn the lessons of the past, did not fully understand the significance of previous conflict, or avoided the mistakes of previous movements. The issue was not a lack of authenticity, or bad intentions but historical blindness. For the resistance to ground itself in a politic of revolution, then it must have an understanding of its own history. Without this understanding it may never have the capacity to insert itself into the larger body politic and the spread capacity to combat the historical injustices that have constituted the nation-state and enabled its survival.

These problems have become quite dire. The resistance, while occasionally militant, remains predominantly focused on protests, and has difficulty rising above them. Every few years the resistance recreates itself, without a conclusive strategic vision, and few revolutionary organizations arise to promote a new direction. Rebels focus on one-off militant demonstrations and the inevitable repression, and then wait for the next go-around, without enough serious thought about where these actions fit in to the larger freedom struggle in the United States or build up organizations capable of seizing territory, overthrowing the State, and abolishing slavery.

Towards Our Struggle

The situation in black America, since the containment of the BLA, is now similar to the 19th century, with huge swathes of the population in bondage, or in some form of penal supervision. With the United States prison system now housing 25% of the world's inmates, the black community has been utterly devastated by mass incarceration. The modern American social system was designed to disguise social problems that have never been addressed since chattel slavery. As Angela Davis puts it:

> From the aftermath of the abolition of slavery, we might take 1865 as that date, until 1877 when Radical Reconstruction was overturned. And it was not only overturned, but it was erased from the historical record. So in the 1960's

we confronted issues that should have been resolved in
the 1860s, one hundred years later. As a matter of fact,
the Ku Klux Klan and the racial segregation that was so
dramatically challenged, during the mid-20th century
freedom movement was produced not during slavery, but
rather in an attempt to manage free black people who would
have otherwise been far more successful...[4]

The sheer magnitude of the prison/slave system has become
a difficult subject for revolutionaries to grapple with due to the
quotidian nature of black suffering.

Individual incidents demonstrate the regularity, and
normality of the cruelty. Jon Burge, a KKK member and police
detective in Chicago, tortured over 120 black men throughout
several decades. He referred to an electric shock device he used
during interrogations as the "nigger box." Prisoner Kevin Moore
was held in Downstate, a penal facility in New York State for
one day before being transferred, and was beaten so badly he
was left with life-threatening injuries, fractured ribs, a collapsed
lung, and facial fractures. One corrections officer scalped Moore's
dreadlocks and decorated his motorcycle with his hair as a trophy.
These horror stories are more the norm than the exception. An
image like the mutilated back of Gordon, the slave who was
whipped and maimed by his slaveowners is analogous to Abner
Louima who was sodomized by the NYPD, iconically being rolled
out of the hospital in a wheel chair, narrowly escaping death due
to his ruptured intestines.

These torture methods do not operate in a vacuum. They
are a reflection, on the level of the individual, of the massive

violence that the US government deploys against the oppressed across the globe. When the US tightened the slave codes, it also expanded the scale of indigenous genocide. While the government exalted its conquest of the indigenous as Manifest Destiny, it also announced the Monroe Doctrine and declared the entire hemisphere its property. After it attacked black rebels in Ferguson, it sent its troops to brutalize the indigenous fighters in Standing Rock. The NYPD proudly perfected its system of institutionalized torture, with Bernard Kerik at the helm of New York City Corrections and later as police commissioner. He subsequently went on to become Interior Minister in Iraq during the US occupation, spearheading the creation of the torture facilities of Abu Ghraib. Under the rubric of global imperialism, the US government exports its homegrown violence from struggle to struggle and then brings new forms of terror back home. The techniques used to terrorize one will eventually terrorize all.

The normalcy of terror is the current political situation in the United States. Depending on the fairness of their skin colors, citizens are regularly deputized, whether as jurors, snitches and police to ensure the black populace doesn't get out of line, and indeed remains on the plantation. As Wilderson observed, white citizens "are not simply 'protected' by the police, they are—in their very corporeality—the police."[5] George Zimmerman is not an anomaly but the norm. The Black Lives Matter uprisings in Ferguson and Baltimore, then must be viewed in light of the Watts Riots or even the Stono Rebellion.

The swing of the counter-revolution is engulfing the entire world. The rise to prominence of the far right around the world,

Golden Dawn, Duterte, ISIS, Le Pen, Britain First, and the coup in Brazil, marks the greatest political shift since WWII. In response to the Black Lives Matter rebellion back home and unstable capitalist accumulation globally, the far right has risen to power in the United States. The far right has seized remarkable amounts of power, and they are wielding it brazenly and recklessly. Acting on decades of xenophobic paranoia, Trump is unleashing the power of the State against Latinos and Muslims, preparing a campaign of ethnic cleansing, detention, and violence. The oppressive apparatus of the American State, constructed through anti-black violence, is now subsuming the country.

The resistance in the United States now has a choice. It must rise beyond the limits of the protest movements that we have become accustomed to and organize revolutionary bodies with the intention of combatting the State, assisting the populace, and expanding our forces both quantitatively and qualitatively.

The Rojava Revolution, the anti-state revolution in northern Syria, provides us with a successful example of the strategies of organization and resistance we need to apply in the US today. This revolution is based on anti-state struggle, feminism, multiplicity, and the ending of ethnic oppression. The revolution is rooted in the Kurdish freedom struggle in the Middle East.

Similar to the Black Panther Party in the US, the Kurds, an oppressed minority group, initially adopted the traditional Marxist-Leninist framework for revolution with a focus towards national liberation, hoping to seize state power and gradually abolish capitalism. At the turn of the century, however, the movement shifted direction and adopted anarchist ideas and reorganized their societies and militant groups so as to render the State obsolete. Furthermore, the Rojava Revolution, while grounded in the ethnic oppression of Kurds, presents a solution that encompasses various ethnicities, religions, and genders.

As the United States marches into darkness, this is where we find the light. We must look at the political situation of the United States today, with all of its barbarism and exploitation, and realize that we are living in a country that is in a political stalemate. The US Civil War was never resolved, and the riots, rebellions, and guerrilla struggles that have taken place since have all attempted to resolve the contradictions that came to a head in the 1860s. The political system is designed for the abasement and degradation of black life; to guarantee that the direct application of force and terror are permanent mainstays of American life. The political system can ensure a great life for some, a troubled life for many, and sheer terror for those it excludes. Today, this system has reached its peak, and the terror that was developed against black life in the United States is being spread throughout the country and around the world in an increasingly erratic fashion.

We must begin to vigorously organize the resistance. From the social centers and workplaces, the prisons and detention centers, in school and homes across the country, we are now launching the Revolutionary Abolitionist Movement. This struggle is a centuries-old conflict, and will not end until we resolve the issues of the Civil War once and for all. A society built on slavery and genocide, and maintained through prison-slavery, is a society that must remain at war with itself. We must fight back now before it is too late. To create a society worth living in we must liberate those in chains from bondage. Those who are seeking escape have the power to liberate those of us who are already engaged in the battle, as we struggle together we build a new world.

What We're Working Towards

Building the revolutionary forces capable of competently engaging in this conflict requires firm grounding in emancipatory political objectives and an understanding of the necessity for militant self-defense. These two components are the preconditions for the expansion of the Abolitionist struggle. The formation of political bodies capable of maintaining cohesion and expansion is paramount, as is the realization that militant actions must be prepared concurrently with and be supplementary to larger political aims.

To rise beyond the limits of protest, we must chart out our political intentions, organizational goals, and a larger vision about our direction. First, and foremost, militant self-defense, and the capacity for larger militant actions must be addressed at the inception of the organizing process. While we must defend people from captivity as well as our political centers, we must also be astute enough to realize that we cannot be on the defense indefinitely. The State is in a weaker position today than it has been in decades, and since the moment we go into action is up to us, the government invariably remains in a defensive position. We can act when we choose and we should act wisely.

Through our actions to liberate those preyed on by the State, our political support will increase. More importantly, our ethical foundation to propose and create a new, and better life will become increasingly more profound. As each participant joins the struggle, their involvement helps defeat the cage of instrumentalized roles, while at the same time, through their participation, the battle against the State is spread throughout society.

The more long-term considerations that are embedded from the beginning, the better our chances will be at turning the resistance into a revolution. If they are set up in a well-considered manner, with new social functions built into their foundations, these networks of resistance can become the communes and councils capable of carving away at state power. The Rojava Revolution provides us with some exemplary attributes that help shape our movement and allow us to trace out the necessary elements of a liberated society. Shared political aspirations are paramount for our success and we propose that the political framework articulated below should become the driving force behind our actions. As we fight for the abolition of the State and the abolition of slavery, we must still maintain fluidity and adapt to the current circumstances, but also retain this larger political purpose.

Our political vision:

1. Self-Defense: The heart of revolutionary transformation

2. Primary unit of self-governance: The neighborhood council

3. Conflict resolution and revolutionary justice

4. Towards the abolition of gender

5. Ownership through use, the co-operative economy and expropriation

Self-Defense:
The heart of revolutionary transformation

> Societies have always adapted and changed in order to defend themselves against attacks. However, with the emergence of the nation-state, self-defense has become part of the monopoly of the State. This monopoly of self-defense includes both military and society. The State has taken on the responsibility of defending its citizens against famine, sickness, poverty and war, but often fails in these duties. Even worse, the State itself is often the main perpetuator of violence against its citizens...[6]
>
> —*Krongeya Star*

The Legacy of Militant Struggle in the Americas

Self-defense is the central pillar of our resistance. The State tries to consolidate its monopoly on violence by claiming to have the unique ability to protect its "citizens," but it has become clear, there is no such thing as protection that one does not provide oneself. Self-defense is not only the barricade against an oppressive force, but also the means for the collective development that is an integral part of revolutionary change. From the bloody inception of the American State, every attempt to subject people under its hegemonic rule has been met with fierce resistance. From the early legacy of indigenous resistance and slave rebellions to later eruptions at Wounded Knee to the rise of the BLA, the drive for liberation has been the central desire of the oppressed.

Maroon societies, in the US South, were autonomous communities of indigenous people, self-freed slaves, and poor whites. They were collective and uncompromisingly committed to defending each other's freedom from slave catchers and bosses. The maroon communities prevented anyone from going without food and protection, and to ensure this, they conducted risky incursions into surrounding areas. Due to the relentless attacks from the government and the planter class, they relied on a fierce backbone of armed defense to maintain their autonomy. Cooperation with nearby maroon communities allowed multiple teams to join together against bigger enemies to create a fluid and powerful fighting force. It was this very decentralized nature of the militias that ensured their autonomy, as well as gave them fighting prowess against a bigger enemy. In fact, during the Civil War they used the same hit and run tactics against the Confederate Army and the plantations.

While the maroons demonstrate the usefulness of localized self-defense of an autonomous region, the resistance in Haiti during the revolution shows the benefits of building a decentralized fighting force from within an imperial society. The history of the resistance consisted of debilitating switch-backs between the two formations that Russell Maroon Shoatz refers to as the "hydra" and the "dragon." When the decentralized forces (the hydra) were unleashed, the resistance enjoyed military success. When a leader centralized the militia and grabbed power (the dragon), they would either be executed by the slavers or imperialists or, as occurred in later years, killed by their own people's resistance due to their despotic behavior.

What is perhaps the most recent example of successful autonomous resistance to the State in the American context was the Black Liberation Army in the early 1970's. Their version of the 'maroon' was an underground network, allowing them to use offensive tactics and prevent infiltration. At their height, they skillfully liberated numerous captive insurgents from state bondage. Against a hegemonic enemy, camouflage was essential. The longer fighters maintained their anonymity, the longer they were able to sustain attacks without taking crippling casualties.

If the Black Liberation Army had been thoroughly tied to a political body before going underground, the political movement in general could have recruited new members through an above-ground organization. By linking such a group with public, council-based organizations founded on liberatory practices, the movement can be built through simultaneously constructing a new way of life and enacting revolutionary justice.

Moreover, the underground model ought to be combined with a visible, aboveground network that delivers both tactical and strategic advantages. Revolutionaries can attract wider community support without forfeiting the benefits of underground organization. The Anti Racist Action (ARA) network in the US in the '80s, '90s, and 2000s carried on the legacy of fighting fascism through a decentralized, militant, above-ground network. Its chapters were grounded locally, with local, anonymous participants driving its activities on the streets. Anti-fascist tactics – focused primarily around the use of physical force—proved effective in forcing neo-Nazi groups out of entire neighborhoods. The tactics were simple, if they came upon a neo-Nazi, they would use sufficient force to drive them away. The network was so successful that it eventually grew to 100 chapters. By joining in a nationwide network, they were able to help spread and strengthen the model while still maintaining local control over each chapter. This model shows the effectiveness of decentralized, locally based activity, reinforced by connective networks across a larger region.

Self-Defense in a Revolutionary Society

Successful self-defense must incorporate revolutionary values and practices. In Rojava, combatants are trained both in fighting techniques and the benefits of creating a feminist, egalitarian society. They put these values into effect through their relationships. For example, to dismantle the lingering effects of patriarchy, no man can give a woman an order; to maintain participation and egalitarian relationships, all fighters contribute to decision-making within units, particularly by selecting their own leaders for specific missions.

The relationships between comrades, born from their own liberation and participation in a bottom-up system, allows them to be very effective militarily. This is hardly surprising, as fighters who believe deeply in the liberatory society they are fighting for, as well as have a profound trust in those around them, are more likely to consistently advance the struggle forward. This strength sustains the integrity of the revolution against its enemies. Through this conscientious method they have built a 50,000-strong militia that has proven to be the most effective force against the Islamic State of Iraq and Syria (ISIS).

The training of these new militants is the revolutionary heart of the Rojava Revolution. The long-term intentions of the training programs are to ensure that everyone can participate in self-defense. To that extent, there are also localized training programs that arm the public for a second tier of neighborhood defense. The Self Defense Forces (HPC*) were formed for this purpose. While specific armed groups, such as the People's Protection Units and Asayîş (YPG** and YPJ*** respectively), have been formed to fight external enemies, the HPC are civilians that get arms training with the specific goal of maintaining autonomy against internal forces that might seek to consolidate power. They are volunteers who receive both political education and self-defense training.

These armed groups are able to defend their communities from attacks without compromising revolutionary values. As the YPG and YPJ liberate ISIS territory new communities become incorporated into their political project. Rather than establish a top-down system of governance, the revolutionary movement establishes new neighborhood councils and communes, feminist education programs, and decentralized local-based militias within each liberated town. To implement this form of political organization, there is undoubtedly a give and take. While the towns receive the infrastructure necessary for self-governance, such as weapons and training from the YPG to set up their own, local defense groups, they agree to uphold certain social principles like feminism and social ecology.

Due to this egalitarian political organization and the relationship engendered through the process the Rojava revolution has not only defended its decentralized political system but has even expanded the council system to neighboring regions.

The core tenets of Rojava's self-defense project are as follows:

- Defense is integral to the growth of the revolutionary movement.

- Militias operate according to liberatory political principles.

---

* HPC or Hêza Parastina Cewherî translates to Civilian Defense Forces.

** YPG or Yekîneyên Parastina Gel translates to People's Protection Units.

*** YPJ or Yekîneyên Parastina Jin translates to Women's Protection Units.

- Within militia units, decision-making is participatory, led from the bottom-up, and leaders are elected during missions.

- Self-defense training is provided to anybody who desires it.

Enhancing Our Struggle

Across the United States, there are currently groups that are committed to the principles of self-defense, from left-wing armed groups to anti-fascist brigades to copwatch organizations. These groups use a variety of tactics and strategies depending on the local conditions, yet they share common enemies: fascists, right-wing militias, and State forces. The groups who have combatted these reactionaries have a proven commitment to defending oppressed communities; they are the foundation upon which we can build a political movement.

Thus, we propose that the existing militant anti-fascist and anti-police movement can be further developed according to the following guidelines:

- Underscoring these groups with a new revolutionary scope and the political principles outlined here.

- Deepening the local scope of these groups by tying the actions to neighborhood self-governance, and a larger political project.

- Connecting these projects to each other to broaden our capacity by increasing resources, participants, and deepening our commitments to revolutionary political solutions.

- Developing the capacity to begin launching offensive actions against fascists and the regime.

Our proposal is to grow locally, while connecting, politically and materially, to similar groups regionally. By placing self-defense at the center of our revolutionary movement, we can protect the development of our political projects and centers. This will allow the values and practices that we are trying to implement to have the opportunity to expand. We propose connecting self-defense groups to the smallest unit of self-governance possible: the neighborhood. This places the capacity for self-defense in the hands of those who need it.

To summarize, we argue:

- Decentralization is an effective militant strategy and shapes the revolutionary practice of defense groups.

- Militant groups are connected to local political bodies organizing towards self-governance.

- Feminism, anti-racism, and the abolition of white supremacy constitute the foundation of defense organizations.

- Core revolutionary principles and goals allow groups to work with a variety of tactics towards the same goal even without direct coordination.

The Neighborhood Council:
Primary unit of self-governance

Building Towards a Council System

When revolutionary groups form projects like the Black Panthers' breakfast programs, the New Orleans based Common Ground Collective, or the Greek anarchists's revolutionary solidarity with Syrian refugees, these initiatives also form new political and social relations based on mutual aid and neighborhood self-sufficiency. Unlike State-based organizations, which turn citizens into helpless recipients of services, volunteer-run projects instead supplied the resources, tools and knowledge for people to provide for themselves, make the primary decisions about organization, and, if firmly tied to self-defense forces, eventually take over the infrastructure necessary for survival.

For example, revolutionary anarchist groups in Athens have been working with refugees from the Syrian Civil War. The refugees are routinely attacked by fascists and often denied housing, food, and health care. Anarchist groups have taken over abandoned hotels and have invited refugees to live in them. However, instead of remaining dependent and trapped in a charity-based relationship, the refugees have organized themselves, in conjunction with anarchists, according to a council-model and now have regular meetings to preside over the allocation of resources to solve their problems communally.

Above all, the Spanish Civil War provides a hallmark example of how emancipatory political principles can be introduced alongside active experimentation with new and innovative forms of self-organization. While conducting the military struggle on the front, militants in the rearguard helped form workers' councils and rural communes, and since anarchists were at the forefront of the struggle, the council-based system was remarkably egalitarian. Workers seized factories, peasants collectivized the land, and even the revolutionary militias were organized in a participatory and non-hierarchical fashion as a result of the anarchist struggle. Indeed, the revolutionary militias were formed in a similarly horizontal manner as the collectives, which reciprocally provided them with both weapons and other provisions. The symbiotic relationship between the worker's councils, collectivized land projects, and horizontal militias demonstrates how the political foundation facilitated cooperation between each of the three organizational structures.

The council system upholds the foundational principles of any resistance movement and sustains the decentralization of power. Importantly, these bodies are directly connected to and have sole jurisdiction over their territory, neighborhood, or town. As the council expands horizontally, its decision-making can be diversified by subdividing into local groups based on specific issues, such as tenants' councils, youth groups, and neighborhood defense units. The implementation of this strategy should, therefore, strive for the three objectives outlined below:

- Revolutionary groups can help found councils grounded in strong political principles.

- The council expands horizontally to new councils and collectives.

- Strengthening connections between councils helps reinforce each one and builds up pragmatic resources and defense.

The Council System in a Revolutionary Society

In Rojava, the neighborhood council is the smallest, most local, and yet most powerful unit of self-governance. The council itself is not a bureaucratic institution. Instead, it is shaped by the people who participate in it. Neighbors meet here to engage in the most immediate form of politics: debating issues, distributing resources, and making decisions. Council members reach solutions to their problems through the active participation. To further empower its members, each council is also subdivided into particular committees based on specific issues. These groups then become the primary actors on issues pertaining their lives.[7]

Since the council system allows for equal participation on the most local level of society, each participant regardless of identity, age, ethnicity, etc, is able to directly affect the conditions of their life. Working with a neighbor when one's life depends on it, creates a fertile ground for trust and mutual concern to grow. When neighbors survive due to their mutual support and cooperation with each other, they are more likely to recognize one another on a human level and care for each other as individuals. The baseless divisions fabricated by the State and perpetuated by the myth of scarcity have no basis here. The process of being politically engaged through the council repels the conditions that result in bigotry, distrust and competition by instead fostering relationships based on understanding.

The decision-making capacity of neighbors in this council system allows people to build autonomous institutions like learning centers, health clinics, and other facilities based on local needs. An example from the autonomous Zapatista region, a precursor to and inspiration for Rojava, illustrates how this process functions. The construction of a hospital in a Zapatista community, called "Madre de los caracoles del mar de nuestros sueños," is a good example of a project developed through the council. Its formation was based on years of conversation between health providers and the people they care for. Due to this dialogue, the resulting hospital reflected the needs of the people in the area. For example, the medicine practiced there ended up being a mixture of local healing arts and traditional western medicine. Health promoters volunteer their time and are supported by the surrounding families, allowing greater focus on people's care instead of working for money. The hospital's quality is affirmed by the fact that it is not only used by people in the nearby community but villagers all around the region.[8]

By imbuing each council with decision-making power, the distribution of governance becomes decentralized and people across a large territory become empowered through the relationships that are forged and the ability to genuinely determine their own living conditions. For instance, returning to the example currently unfolding in Rojava, it has been collectively mandated that no other council or regional body is allowed to override its decisions, making the local council becomes the most powerful unit. The core of these revolutionary bodies are built through the minutia of day-to-day interactions, and through the individual realization that when a person has overthrown oppression in the most intimate fashion, and now lives a self-actualized life, a return to conventional, day-to-day despotism will not occur without a fight.

Towards Our Struggle

The political paradigm we are working towards is a network of councils and communes without the State. It's a vision of autonomy that runs through neighborhood-based councils, where decision-making rests at the local level. This political formation reverses hierarchy and centralized power by making the most local unit the most powerful, and regional bodies simply a means for coordination. We propose starting from the nexus of the small, revolutionary groups already active in many cities, towns, and rural areas. Already, such groups function as local political collectives with strong ethical backbones and a commitment to communal decision-making.

As these groups expand through the abolitionist struggle, they have the ability to introduce more people to this model of politics. The purpose, then, is to expand qualitatively and quantitatively, without recreating centralized and hierarchical social formations. To facilitate the process of liberating people from bondage, we offer the following suggestions as possible means by which revolutionary groups can help establish structurally decentralized projects that integrate uncompromising anarchist foundations through the creation of new councils and local institutions:

- Revolutionary groups can create social programs, such as a free health clinics, safe houses for immigrants and others targeted by the State, educational programs, etc., with a revolutionary outlook, in order to bring new people into new revolutionary methods of organization, while building localized resources.

- They can help form new collectives and councils, based on either local circumstances or a specific issue, such as tenants' associations, revolutionary youth groups, or neighborhood assemblies.

- Revolutionary groups can build stronger relationships with similar groups in other cities.

The success of this project is measured by more and more people within a neighborhood becoming politically engaged and active decision-makers within their communities. While the State drags on by using increasingly totalitarian methods, we build our power: building new communities of resistance in the disintegrating remains of the regime. By proliferating, these bodies can, in the short term, erode the oppressive functions of the State, and partnered with rigorous defense, dislodge them.

Conflict Resolution and Revolutionary Justice

Revolutionary Justice

The legacy of revolutionary justice in the US is an inherently political phenomenon, as it has always been situated in reprisals against the State, the slave-holding planter class, capitalists and their institutions, and the broader forces of bondage, from colonial to patriarchal oppression. It is impossible to speak about resolving social conflicts in the US without addressing the agents of the State and reactionary, racist forces, and their consistent use of terror to maintain their social and political position.

Revolutionary justice may just as easily be called self-defense. In fact, the oppressed are often left with no other option: given the brutal, methodical, and continued nature of their subjugation. Their only choice for survival is to strike back. This distinct mode of defensive attack is epitomized in the legacies of Nat Turner and John Brown. After rallying a formidable group of rebels, Nat Turner's armed formation went from plantation to plantation, killing plantation owners and freeing slaves. With his militant band of abolitionists, John Brown put up a valiant armed resistance to pro-slavery militias in Kansas before launching his famous assault on the federal armory at Harper's Ferry from which he intended to get weapons to distribute to slaves for their rebellion. These actions were selfless attempts to free people, and were conducted explicitly on the side of the oppressed. The profound level of violence universally used by the slaveholders meant that only an equivalent level of violence would suffice for liberation.

Revolutionary justice was administered in a more organized fashion by maroon communities in their targeted attacks on the planter class. For example, the maroon called the Great Dismal Swamp became the epicenter slave emancipation. Some 2,000 fugitives fled to the swamp including debt fugitives, ex-slaves, and refugees from the brutal wars on the indigenous populations, creating autonomous communities of resistance. The maroon societies were not satisfied with just their own liberty; they rose up to fight for others as well. Their numbers grew as they attacked plantations and liberated slaves. Their original attacks took place in the regions bordering the swamp. However, as intercepted communications show, the maroon communities intended to attack entire towns to destroy the system of power that sustained the slave system.[9]

Every prison uprising from Attica* to Lucasville**, is an example of revolutionary justice. Every group that goes

---

* During the Attica Prison Riot in 1971, about 1,000 of the Attica prison's approximately 2,200 inmates rioted and took control of the prison, taking 42 staff hostage for 4 days.

** The Lucasville Uprising was a rebellion against oppressive and racist policies at the Southern Ohio Correctional Facility (SOCF) in Lucasville, OH in 1993. Nine inmates and one guard died during the uprising. Many people are currently serving time or condemned to death by the State of Ohio in relation to the uprising.

underground to launch clandestine attacks against bondage
and oppression, like the Black Liberation Army or the United
Freedom Front*, engages in acts of revolutionary justice. The
uprisings of the 1960s in Watts, Newark, and Detroit, to the
Los Angeles riots, and the recent insurrections in Ferguson and
Baltimore sparked by executions from police are manifestations
of revolutionary justice.

No platform, no dialogue, no inch of territory, and certainly
no concern can be ceded to those who either threaten or
unleash authoritarian, white supremacist violence. As the Italian
anarchist, Alfredo M. Bonanno has eloquently put it, "The life of
someone who oppresses others and prevents them from living is
not worth a cent."[10]

When a person chafes under the subjugation of violent
oppression, and breaks away from it, whether as part of a
revolutionary group, an organized society, or simply as a lone
actor, this is an act of revolutionary justice. The methods of this
justice are a far cry from the methods we reserve for those within
our revolutionary groups, and our own communities. This line
is clearly demarcated by the division between the oppressed
versus the oppressor. For the oppressor, we have nothing but
antagonism and struggle; for the oppressed, we have nothing but
understanding and compassion.

---

* The United Freedom Front (UFF) was a small Marxist organization active
in the Northeast in the 1970s and 1980s. They targeted corporate buildings,
courthouses, and military facilities.

Conflict Resolution in a Revolutionary Society

The entire council-based system, as in Spain, Chiapas, or Rojava, is predicated on the health of the social fabric. All pragmatics, education, and values are collectively organized so that the individual can overcome alienation and powerlessness by personally shaping the conditions of their lives through discussion and decision-making. The ability to shape all the facets of society confers upon each individual a far wider scope than the mere satisfaction of personal needs, as it also includes the well-being of the entire community. With the invisible wall between politics and community broken down, this focus on community health becomes the driving force behind the process of resolving conflicts. If we intend to resolve the conflicts between parties instead of simply finding fault and applying punishment, the solution is mediation. In Rojava, conflict resolution is implemented in several, slightly different ways throughout the society that the participants are actively involved in constructing.

The Tekmil

The Tekmil is a foundational process that begins with self-reflection and analysis based on revolutionary principles. In fact, it's important to note that this practice is what led to this region's transition from a hierarchical national liberation struggle to its current ground-up structure.

The Tekmil is implemented in all organizations from the YPG/YPJ militias to all revolutionary organs in civil society. The main point is that each person 'criticizes' those they care the most about because they want to see them improve and become better people. To begin on a serious footing, the participants step into another room, and act as if those fallen in the struggle are there with them. Thus, people are expected to act respectfully. There's typically a person that leads the Tekmil and writes down the criticisms, who starts by opening the floor up to anyone that has something to say. If a person feels the need to express themselves, they ask if they can speak, stand up and give their observations. If they're speaking about someone else, that person cannot reply to their criticism. In fact, they are not even supposed to bring it up after the Tekmil. They are just supposed to accept it and think about it. Once no one has anything else to say, the person leading the Tekmil summarizes what was stated.

For the newly enlisted, there is a general Tekmil held every three days in addition to a session conducted after every military training and political education class This allows the potential for hierarchy between the trainers and trainees to stop from forming, as trainees are constantly given the opportunity to criticize them and their approaches to instruction. In addition to summarizing their observations of what occurred during the Tekmil, the trainers also conclude by stating how they can make certain desired changes and improvements. This is intended to be a harmonizing process, a reminder of what the revolutionary horizon is, and how everyone can work on themselves to stay on point.[11]

The Peace and Consensus Committee

In Rojava conflict resolution is handled in a bottom-up manner and integrated into daily life as opposed to exclusively institutional settings. At the level of the neighborhood, participation in the commune or committees is already a preventative measure. People generally are already invested in the well-being of their counterparts, due to the process of working through social issues locally. When a conflict occurs, people are more invested in finding a solution due to the organizational process. The more developed the revolutionary project becomes, then, the more successful conflict resolution will become.

The Peace and Consensus Committee is composed of a few neighbors who are invested in finding a reasonable outcome to conflicts. The "office" where they meet is a neighbor's house. The family might be at home, other neighbors may pop in, and in the middle of this familiar environment, the participants talk over the issue they are trying to resolve. According to Ercan Ayboğa, "The goal of Peace and Consensus Committees…is not to condemn one or both sides in a proceeding but rather to achieve a consensus between the conflicting parties. If possible, the accused is not ostracized through a punishment or locked away but rather is made to understand that his or her behavior has led to injustice, damage, and injury. If necessary, the matter is discussed for a long time. Reaching consensus among the parties is a result that will lead to a more lasting peace."[12] This means that every party must be committed to enacting the solution, rather than merely agreeing heartlessly to it, or worse, being bureaucratically, and indifferently, coerced into compliance.

Work of the Council

Another good example of how these methods work is in the councils of Bakur, or Southeastern Turkey, which preceded the revolution in Rojava. Here there is a dual-power situation: revolutionary councils exist even though the State has not been abolished. "When we talk about judicial matters, you have to understand that we're trying to organize a society without a State. Many people who have legal disputes or other problems that need solving don't go to the Turkish courts anymore-they come to the city councils."[13]

Council members will sit down with people in the midst of a crisis and talk it through with them. According to one council member, "We work with conversation, dialogue, negotiation, and when necessary, criticism and self-criticism. When someone does something wrong, the party who perpetuated the harm has to make it up to the people he injured...There's no death penalty, we don't put perpetrators in prison or penalize them financially." Even in cases as serious as murder, the solution is to help the perpetrator develop into a better person, using the help of psychologists or others.

There is an extraordinary precedent set by this situation. A council-member's priority is not a bureaucratic process of instituting law, but instead, personally working with those who need it.

The exact format and process of such solutions vary, as they should, depending on the needs or relationships of each neighborhood. What they have in common is that those who will be affected by the decision are always the ones who propel the process, and there is a wholehearted commitment to mending the social fabric rather than punishment.

How conflict resolution works:

- Social cohesion, not punishment, is the intended result.

- The process must be predicated on the personal development of those involved.

- The people affected by the decisions drive the process, and all parties must agree with the resolution.

- Conflict resolution works best when coupled with strong, continuous relationships between participants.

- Liberatory political principles must be the criteria for all resolutions.

Towards Our Struggle

Revolutionary justice is an unpredictable, yet inevitable, element in revolutionary struggle. As we move towards liberation, there will be spontaneous eruptions, moments to support and side with, as well as alliances to create. The more power tries to suppress the population, the more defiant the acts of revolutionary justice become. No one can bear an oppressive situation forever. Both the riot and the lone attack have recently become common. Both are expressions of a need for a radically different social arrangement, but neither has the capacity to deliver long-term solutions. Like the rebellions of Nat Turner and John Brown, these can easily be subdued and crushed without infrastructure, support, and connections to revolutionary political movements.

When police killed Michael Brown in Ferguson, the town erupted in riots. No sooner had they begun this act of defiance, when non-profits and faith "leaders" descended upon the town to induce people to protest "peacefully" and attempted to de-escalate the situation. On the other hand, riot police and armed right-wing militias surrounded the rebels, cornered them in a sea of "illegality" by declaring curfews, and then swept people up with brutal arrests and long jail terms. Without revolutionary objectives, or the foundations for a sustained revolutionary conflict, everyone had to, eventually, reconcile living with the oppressive State that they were just rebelling against when the riot subsided.

The most essential tasks are to create the ideological underpinnings for revolt and the necessary infrastructure that can sustain action and long-term forms of organization.

There is a big difference materially in what an organized and fortified hamlet versus a mass in revolt can accomplish. With a base of operations impenetrable to outsiders, the maroons were able to provide a serious challenge to the practitioners of slavery. Tactically, they leveraged the advantage of attack from a free area outside the jurisdiction of hegemonic power. However, it was not only their territorial integrity, but a commitment to the autonomous nature of their societies that allowed for the maroon's perseverance. The maroons refused to give up their freedoms, maintained regional decision-making and fluid fighting formations, and continued traditional practices. Outsiders looking for liberation saw that the people involved in maroon communities weren't struggling to grab power, but to fight for liberation itself.

In this regard, an overarching political objective is also absolutely necessary. In order to go on the offensive, groups need a foundational reason to act, to liberate individuals, to liberate new territories, or weaken the State. Revolutionary communities must exemplify the new socio-political relationships that they seek to create in society at large. The Black Liberation Army articulated a compelling political perspective which made its actions legible to a broader community, and situated revolutionary justice within a political tradition.

Where the BLA was hampered by not having an aboveground organization to bring people in, anarchist activity during the Spanish Civil War provides a great example of how a public organization combined with defense forces can better integrate oppressed populations. After storming a barrack, anarchists freed all the prisoners. Political prisoners were locked up there and had been talking with other prisoners about the revolution. Many of these captives had already been radicalized by their abusive jailers and saw the ideas presented as a transformative option. Upon release, these newly politicized prisoners were ready to participate in the political model of their rescuers. Many of them joined the movement as part of the Iron Column, putting into practice revolutionary relationships and organization, while fighting against oppressive forces. Their militia had a fluid and egalitarian nature, which was itself an active example of the organizational forms it fought for.

Through this example, it is possible to see how building upon revolutionary relationships and political objectives can add weight and longevity to inevitable eruptions against oppressive forces. Were it not for the strength of the relationships between militia members, it would have been difficult for revolutionaries to face a powerful external enemy during the Spanish Civil War. Maintaining internal social cohesion and building revolutionary organization turns sporadic revolutionary justice into a comprehensive political force. By laying proper political frameworks both in terms of practice and ideology, revolutionary groups today have the capacity to turn the tide of spontaneous revolt into something that can sustain itself. If successful, we will inspire others to acts of revolutionary justice and self-liberation, initiating participation in building the political foundations of the future. The revolution will build the revolution.

There are four important ways revolutionary groups can contribute to such moments:

- Look to the communities that are most oppressed for comrades in struggle.

- Fight alongside and defend groups enacting revolutionary justice.

- Derail forces that want to bring people back into the fold of power: nonprofits, political parties, and authoritarian political groups.

- Provide political foundations: principles, new organizational models, infrastructure and defense.

Towards the Abolition of Gender

The patriarchal control and the relation of terror that engenders slavery, and sets the conditions for modern political reality in the US, is truly exemplified in the social position of the female slave. The remarkably cruel degree of control exercised on black women embodies the violence of the reproductive process that constitutes black life. While patriarchal violence is a phenomenon that is ubiquitous, when coupled with the slave system, the oppression becomes exceptionally totalizing and creates a uniquely onerous web of violence.

Black life was, as it is now, constituted through foundational violence; the slave relation rendered black people as non-people. The issue here is not that people were not given rights, but that a substantial part of the public was not considered human, so the formation of "man," or "woman," has a different meaning within this context. Motherhood, for instance, was crucial in reproducing property for slave society. Furthermore, parental rights were non-existent, children were sold and separated from families at will and children were renamed to ensure patriarchal domination by the slaveowner. Afro-pessimist author Saidiya Hartman argues:

> The captive female does not possess gender as much as she is possessed by gender that is, by way of a particular investment in and use of the body. What "woman" designates in the context of captivity is not to be explicated in terms of domesticity or protection but in terms of the

disavowed violence of slave law, the sanctity of property and the necessity of absolute submission, the pathologizing of the black body, the restriction of black sentience, the multifarious use of property, and the precarious status of the slave within the public sphere.[14]

It is under this reign of terror that the category of "women" as it operates generally in United States was constructed on the basis of the total captivity of black women. Gender roles in the US are situated within this context; the normalization of the white family unit and its categories of woman and man can't be extricated from the ownership relation. If we desire to create a world where this fixed categorization is abolished, where heteronormativity is dismantled, and people can truly create themselves without the imposition of coercive and prefabricated roles, then we must begin the struggle at the origin of the non-human/human relations, the relations of terror, and the patriarchal relation of property.

The destruction of the gender binary and the liberation from patriarchal control, then, must be based off a politic of action. The foundational violence that established the human/non-human, man/woman, or slave/free dichotomies is constructed through the process of captivity and terror. We must destroy the means of captivity, and political infrastructure that makes the reign of terror possible. By destroying the material means of captivity, we can begin reconfiguring the categorization of captive gender roles. We can begin this process through revolutionary organization and self-defense which is crucial at this juncture.

From Self-Emancipation to Organization

Emancipatory struggles that have the potential to overturn normative relations and open realms of social and political possibilities have customarily materialized from movements and revolutionary organizations that focused on destroying the mechanisms of captivity. Furthermore, the autonomous action of rebel women have often been tied into militant political projects that help expand the potential of feminist politics. There are numerous historical examples that indicate how the war against patriarchy in the United States has always been tied to the struggle against the slave-system and its interconnected network of property relations.

For instance, Harriet Tubman made gallant contributions to the early abolitionist struggle by liberating slaves from captivity, and gained even greater success as her actions became tied into the larger struggle for liberation on a national scale. Her life exemplified the necessity of resistance and self-defense. A working slave since five years old, she suffered greatly and witnessed the destruction of her family.

Harriet Tubman's journey from bondage is the prototype of revolutionary action. She refused to stay in captivity any longer exclaiming, "[T]here was one of two things I had a right to... liberty or death; if I could not have one, I would have the other." Seeing no option except self-defense, she escaped via the informal underground railroad network and then became one of its strongest participants, freeing her own family and seventy others over a decade. Tubman was always armed with a revolver for self-defense during passage. Her work culminated in helping

John Brown organize the Harper's Ferry assault, recruiting runaway slaves for the action, attaining the name "General Tubman," in the process. Lastly, Tubman was the first woman to head an armed expedition during the Civil War, as she guided the raid at Combahee Ferry, which liberated 750 slaves.[15]

Tubman's escape from the plantation was crucial for her self-liberation. This first step, not by patronage, but by action, challenged not just the patriarchal foundations of the slave-system, but also helped escalate the war against the State by strengthening the underground network. When she took that step, she regained control of herself as a woman and as a human being, and in so doing, garnered the confidence to free others. With the remarkable degree of fortitude to overcome the mentality of one victimized by slave relations, she at one and the same time rejected bondage and patriarchy.

The totalizing violence and dehumanization imposed through the slave-system overcome personally by Tubman, and by the liberated slaves in general, marked a break from the human/non-human relation. Once liberated, she did not slip into the constrictive roles offered by "womanhood" in "free" society; her work threw into question gender roles themselves. As she traversed the underground railroad, her confidence inspired others to free themselves; and her actions culminated in her great raid at Combahee Ferry, where she demonstrated the revolutionary understanding that individual freedom necessitates the destruction of the system in its entirety, and the freedom of all.

Approximately a century after Tubman's courageous actions, Black Liberation Army combatant, Assata Shakur continued the resistance struggle against captivity and slave society. Shakur had been an organizer with the Black Panther Party in New York City in the Harlem branch, and actively participated in the larger black liberation struggle. The State, in a brazen display of arrogance, attempted to pin every bank robbery or violent crime committed by a black woman on Shakur. The intense repression of the black liberation movement during COINTELPRO culminated for Shakur with a shootout on the New Jersey Turnpike, where her closest friend Zayd Shakur was killed, and she and her comrade Sundiata Acoli were detained.

The cruel treatment Shakur had to endure in the hands of the State is emblematic of the sheer barbarism of US slave-society. Shakur was initially housed in solitary confinement for 21 months and then moved to a maximum-security facility that housed several white supremacists. Later she was transferred to another facility where she was routinely brutalized.

The State's intentions were obvious from the outset: they intended to punish her for fighting for general liberation and reaffirm its dominance through her subjugation. She personally observed the integral connection between bondage, race, and patriarchy. During her time in prison she concluded, "There are no criminals here at Riker's Island Correctional Institution for Women, (New York), only victims. Most of the women (over 95%) are black and Puerto Rican. Many were abused children. Most have been abused by men and all have been abused by 'the system.'"[16]

Her BLA comrades organized her heroic escape from prison and after a period of living underground, helped her escape to Cuba where she still lives today. The US government, in its longstanding commitment to black captivity and white supremacy, has gone to extreme lengths to bring her back, placing a $2 million dollar bounty on her head, put her on the top list of most wanted terrorists, and pressured the Cuban government to extradite her to the US.

Like Harriet Tubman, her path of escape and resistance began to change the narrative of resistance movements, and of political reality. It is through this path of resistance and organization that we see these women recreate themselves and what liberation could look like for others. So when Shakur proclaims, "I am a 20th century escaped slave," she reconstitutes the struggle for abolition to its original place in US politics, and the original incarceration of womanhood. She herself understood the necessity for total emancipation, saying, "Women can never be free in a country that is not free. We can never be liberated in a country where the institutions that control our lives are oppressive... Or while the amerikan government and amerikan capitalism remain intact."[16]

The fight for women's liberation then is acutely tied to the destruction of the patriarchal social relations that were established by the totalizing terror of slavery. The liberation of one woman is dependent on the liberation of all so if even one woman liberates herself from captivity, the potential for the destruction of the US system is that much more likely. This explains the outrageous response to Shakur's liberation and this is why the State cannot tolerate seeing its captives freed, particularly when they are freed on their own terms. Yet the inverse is much more crucial: that as more women take it upon themselves to actively and militantly participate in their own emancipation, the destruction of the State becomes immanent, and with its demise, the carceral nature of gender roles codified by it begins to unravel. As Assata Shakur encourages us:

> Under the guidance of Harriet Tubman and Fannie Lou Hamer and all of our foremothers, let us rebuild a sense of community. Let us rebuild the culture of giving and carry on the tradition of fierce determination to move on closer to freedom.[16]

Feminism in a Revolutionary Society

In other revolutionary periods around the world we find organized forces that coalesced around feminist militancy. In many of these instances, organization took on expansive forms that led to both challenging gender normalization and unlocking revolutionary possibilities.

During the Spanish Civil War, for example, the powerful female militia Mujeres Libres took up the dual call of self-defense and self-emancipation. In their words:

> We did not want to substitute a feminist hierarchy for a masculine one. It's necessary to work, to struggle, together because if we don't we'll never have a social revolution. But we needed our own organization to struggle for ourselves.[17]

They combined self-activity with direct action, putting into practice pragmatic steps for liberation, and making revolution a reality. In addition to laying the political groundwork by building numerous organizational projects - from education to infrastructure, they provided support for women in the militias, setting up shooting ranges and target practice classes. The direct link between action, education, and new organizational forms allowed them to facilitate broad new social life, expanding to 30,000 members. By building new organizations, based completely on a new social outlook, they were able to create a more functional, liberatory society.

In Rojava, restructuring gender roles begins with how knowledge is produced. The political goal of their feminist education system is to overcome the hierarchy of knowledge and to change the nature of science and education. "We aim to understand the mechanisms that lay at the basis of the dominance of men's language and of the exclusion of women from the history of this field by understanding the politics of power and truth regimes." To counterbalance the truth regimes that reinforce patriarchal power, organizations like Kongreya Star realized what was needed was a study that originates from women's perspectives. This comes in the form of, what the Kurdish freedom movement calls, Jineology, which is essentially the re-making of social sciences from the female perspective.

This is implemented pragmatically by a parity between women's and men's participation in social life. Across all aspects of life, from the Councils to the militia, to civic roles to co-operatives, there is a women's only component to complement the same of men or mixed gender. To enter any of the armed groups, trainees must first receive education on revolutionary principles, specifically Jineology. Because patriarchy is so deeply rooted, historically, their solution is to not only seek parity for women but to give women a higher footing. So while the armed group the YPG is all genders, the YPJ is female only. While engaged in militia activity men are not allowed to give women orders in any circumstance. A House of Women in each town gives training to men and women on women's rights, and participates in advanced conflict mediation that pertain to women. The development of collectives is aided by Aboriya Jin, specifically to help women's co-operatives get off the ground. As a result, women in Rojava have taken control of their lives in new ways, from healthcare to education to mediation, as well as three separate defense forces and an independent economic body.

This systematic practice of centering women, from re-making formative social sciences to creating a culture where women live with a higher degree of self-direction and autonomous self-defense proved indispensable when armed units from the Islamic State in Iraq and Syria (ISIS) enslaved women who were on the periphery of Rojava's social revolution. In August 2014, ISIS attacked Yezidi villages in the Sinjar region of Iraq, driving locals into the mountains. They bulldozed villages, captured thousands of women, forcing them into sex slavery and slaughtered over 5,000, making this one of the most recent acts of genocide in the world. As the survivors taking refuge on Sinjar Mountain were surrounded by ISIS, they were abandoned by state military. It was the feminist forces of the YPG/YPJ who took the initiative to fight ISIS back.

Expanding on the liberatory organization in Rojava, the Yezidis were assisted in establishing their own self-defense forces and organs of self-governance. Sex slaves rescued by feminist militias, have become the fighters of the YJÊ, the Yezidi Women's

Units, turning their dehumanization and victimhood into the pinnacle of resistance. The transformation through self-defense led to the YJÊ and its mixed-gender counterpart to re-take ground from ISIS, including the city of Sinjar less than a year after the genocide, and continuing to liberate their friends and family still in captivity. "For the first time in our history, we take up arms because with the last massacre, we understood that nobody will protect us; we must do it ourselves,"[18] proclaimed a YJÊ fighter. The totalizing violence that almost engulfed Yezidi women in their entirety, condemning them to the slave-relations previously discussed, was destroyed by and transformed into armed women's self-defense.

Towards Our Struggle

We must integrate a comprehensive project to permanently dislodge, and destroy the apparatuses of control that have made slave-society and patriarchal control possible. Two immediate courses of action to achieve this outcome are to tie pragmatic feminism into the larger abolitionist framework whose main pragmatic purpose is to help those fleeing oppressive situations and state repression, while forming a militant wing to help protect this political project.

With each revolutionary project outlined above we can see how this process could work in our context. In revolutionary Spain and Rojava militants established a liberatory political framework that necessitates having women's liberation at its core. In each of these processes it was essential for women to organize self-defense teams autonomously. In revolutionary Spain, Mujeres

Libre organized over 30,000 women. While the YPJ in Rojava has trained a remarkably expansive fighting force for and by women. Putting self-defense at the core of the revolutionary process has the potential to build strength and uproot stagnant roles. From Harriet Tubman to the YPJ, female fighting forces have always built the strongest revolutionary projects.

The process of undoing gender roles can be viewed as similar to the process of dismantling the carceral state. Putting self-defense at the origin of this process has the potential of both building strength and uprooting stagnant roles. Whether we look at Harriet Tubman and the Underground Railroad or YJÊ in Sinjar, when people have the opportunity to autonomously defend themselves, and fight for others, the normativity of fixed identities are called into question, and the process of abolishing gender, and creating a fluid world of self-determination becomes possible. This opening necessitates larger political organization. With revolutionary defense tied to the origins of this project we can begin fighting for the diffusion of power, and as power is diffused, new possibilities arise with a proliferation of identities. Within the abolitionist framework, feminism and queer struggle becomes rooted in a historical politic of liberation.

It is clear that neither victimization nor the constrictive gender roles power thrives on, should be tolerated much longer. Anarchists and other revolutionary groups have already began self-defense classes, queer gun clubs, and rapid response networks for trans people. By tying these projects to a broader revolutionary mission, multiplying their efforts by training new complementary units, placing them at the center of social organizations and creating the avenues for mutual support, we can build viable self-defense and the capacity to release others from bondage.

It is through organizing defense and relating these activities to the larger abolitionist framework that we can begin to really grapple with the relation of terror in US society, patriarchal domination, and the expanding slave-system. Those who deeply understand its carceral mechanisms are the ones who will best be able to defeat them.

Ownership Through Use:
The Co-operative Economy and Expropriation

Expropriation and Collectivity

Revolutionary struggle necessitates an aspiration for collectivity. Those who exploit us and withhold the fruits of our work from us will not willingly give up their wealth and power. To carve out autonomous territory, or to begin the revolutionary process, goods, land, and tools must be expropriated, or taken away from those who withhold them.

The strategy of expropriation has historical roots in the Abolitionist struggle. It was used directly following the Emancipation Proclamation as a means to destroy the system of plantation labor and to hinder the capacity of the planter class as they fought to reintroduce slavery in the US. Plantations were pillaged, while plantation property and records destroyed. In another case, the land at a Georgia plantation was subdivided by and parceled out to former slaves for their cultivation.

For expropriation to be a successful tactic political organizations must already be in place. As goods and production are taken over, they can be put into collective hands, and organized for communal use. During the Spanish Civil War, workplaces were seized after the owners fled or stopped production to sabotage the revolution. Revolutionaries continued until all major places of work were taken over; many were run and controlled by the workers. In others committees were established to override a lingering boss. In the most ideal cases, decisions were made collectively through an assembly, and delegates would deal with everyday issues.

This didn't happen spontaneously. Radical union members were already organized or had become ensconced in these workplaces, which ensured that they would take on these roles. It's also important to note that these cooperatives relied on the political momentum sweeping across all levels of society, as in the militias, schools, food distribution, and so on. Without this wave of social liberation, it would have been difficult to protect workplace seizures or ensure collectivity.

Ownership by Use and a Cooperative Economy

In Rojava, the metric for deciding who gets what is not who can pay the most, but what needs people have. Resources produced locally are primarily for the people who live there, and the intention is equal distribution throughout the communes. The intention is "ownership by use" rather than ownership for the sake of profit. For example, homelessness does not exist because whoever needs a home can use an empty one, and communal relations, and familial ties ensure people have this basic necessity. The neighborhood councils help facilitate the distribution of food and necessities, making sure health and sustenance are provided broadly.

Production happens through non-hierarchical co-operatives. To make sure that women are equally represented, organizations such as the Women's Economic Committee provides training on how to set up and run a co-operative: "In a capitalist economy, the person with the expertise becomes the owner and extracts profit from employing other people. Our system is not capitalist—people work together on a basis of equality and share the resources equally on the basis of solidarity. Everybody acquires expertise so they are self-reliant."[19]

This economic model is ideal for both encouraging self-direction and regional self-sufficiency. Food production in the autonomous territory of the Zapatistas shows how these principles can be integrated. The Zapatista food system is developed according to the perspective that residents and the local food system are intertwined. Food and knowledge production are guided by the necessity of preserving the health and well-being of individuals, communities, and ecosystems. Agricultural students are taught sustainable farming methods that promote autonomy through communal subsistence farming, collectivizing harvests, and equitably distributing labor. Here the economic system and the ideological and social are virtually indistinguishable from one another and are adapted for communal life.

Towards the struggle

Those who strive for liberation typically have a drive toward communalization. On the one hand, when the immediate desire for liberation erupts in riots, looting routinely results in communalizing the bounty in the streets. In these moments of rupture, the default tendency of self-organization usually results in collectivity and sharing. On the other, a number of revolutionary groups around the country have already begun building the basis of a co-operative economy.

For those already committed to communality, from die-hard organizers to sympathetic donors, there is consistently selfless donation to revolutionary movements in the form of time, resources, and expropriated goods. Whatever the level of engagement, there is always genuine motivation that underpins this generosity. These people are not trying to get paid or seek personal fame, but are deeply invested in the outcome of the movement and will commit their resources to as best they can. At the same time, they are constructing the infrastructure for communal resources.

Even without direct coordination, incidents can rouse massive amounts of money, as in when a comrade is injured during a battle. With more circumspection and careful planning, collectives like Anarchist Black Cross, which supports political prisoners, have built substantial commissary funds, while others have built collective warchests. This foundation can be expanded to the broader public through programs like the Black Panthers' Survival Programs, where free meals and clothing, free stores, health clinics, and other resources were made available to the broader public. This effort established an economy based on mutual aid and builds up the health and well-being of people in areas excluded from basic necessities by the State.

In a more recent example, the Anti-Repression Committee in San Francisco began as a means for bailing movement members out of jail after political actions. The fund was started by an original set of donations. Members bail people out using that money and once the person returns to court, the money recycles back to the fund. The Committee became a useful way of supporting everyone participating in the resistance as well as distributing funding to the most needy cases.

This economy was expanded when the Anti-Repression Committee began tracking down and paying the bail of people who had joined a protest for the first time. As they were not known to long-time revolutionaries, these people could easily have fallen through the cracks of support. The Committee connected with scouts in the legal response community who would give them a heads up when such a person was arrested. By extending the fund in this way, people new to the movement were initiated into the practice of mutual aid and movement support. They were invited into the community and made to feel that their rebellion didn't carry the stigma of arrest, but would, in fact, be aided if they chose to continue participating.

As a resistance movement, our ability to provide for ourselves is relative to our territorial expansion. In conjunction with carving out enclaves, expropriation is an important move as we create political spheres by establishing communities of resistance. The basis of such an economy will be returning land and its material resources to the hands of the people who live there, and communalizing resources amongst neighbors.

In the immediate future, the success of struggles based on the same political foundations is essential for the growth of all of them. This horizontal network must be built through strong political allegiances, based on established networks and extended to the ones that we will soon build. Revolutionary groups and councils activate material resources, and move them from areas of abundance to regions of need. By expanding these practices to our neighbors, they in turn open up access to new resources. Mutual support cuts through borders and the artificial deprivation of capitalism, increasing our ability to expand.

In Conclusion

Revolutionary change will not come as a singular event, nor an immediate exchange of power, but an ongoing struggle to free us all from the bonds of oppression and distribute power to communities of resistance. The illusion that a small group can seize state power and enact the will of the majority has dried up in the gulags, prisons, and killing fields of nation-states around the world. The Cantons of Rojava, a network of councils without the State, has introduced a new revolutionary paradigm.

The organization is simple and pragmatic: resources are distributed to people based on need and decisions are made by those they affect. Yet the councils solve many larger problems by negating the role of domination and hierarchy in political relationships. The ability of revolutionary organization, tied into decentralized political practices, to free the most oppressed members of our society has shown that it is the key to victory in our centuries-long struggle for liberation.

Within the scope of the abolitionist struggle, it is essential to work towards a long term liberatory solution. The legacy of previous struggles in the US demonstrates that our need for new methods of revolutionary organization must be built deliberately, completely outside the carceral apparatus of the State, and grounded in the predominant conflicts in the country. Our project's integrity depends on whether it is rooted in destroying the slave-state, revolutionary decentralization, and vigorous self-defense to prevent other political forces from subsuming or defeating us.

As we formulate our next steps, we harken to Rojava as a model. Just as it is grounded in the Kurdish liberation movement in Rojava, we here must ground ourselves in the black liberation movement against slavery. We must organize locally in the council model and protect and expand our work with militant self defense. Lastly, as the Kurds fought against slavery in Sinjar, we must destroy the slave system in the US. By outlining the next steps of our struggle with this revolutionary formulation in mind, we can find a way to carry our indomitable struggle forward.

A Revolutionary Abolitionist Movement

With the stroke of a pen the US managed to abolish slavery while re-instituting it at the same time. In 1865 the US ratified the 13th Amendment of the Constitution, establishing the notion that "slavery" and "involuntary servitude" were permitted as "punishment for crime." Today we are living with that legacy. It is a legacy of servitude and genocide, of patriarchal violence and enclosure, of pain and suffering. We must not forget, however, that we have a legacy of resistance. Our struggles in the 19th century brought the country to its knees, but instead of earnestly attempting to resolve the question of anti-black dehumanization and native genocide, the government chose to retrench its position. This is why we must rebuild our previous strength, orient our strategies for the present, and rekindle the flame of abolition.

When we speak of abolitionism we are not harkening back to a time with no relation to the present. Rather, we are acknowledging our lineage in this struggle. The Revolutionary Abolitionist Movement in the 21st century, then, must recognize the mistakes of previous conflicts, make adjustments, and broaden our sights so that counter-revolutionary forces cannot steal our victories, and so we aren't outmaneuvered. After the Civil War, northern abolitionists were content with the Union victory and applauded themselves and the country for abolishing chattel slavery. Black people in the South began building progressive institutions but were left defenseless against the counter-revolutionary onslaught. There may not have been a concrete strategy that would have beat back Andrew Johnson and the planter class, but it is clear the reliance on US forces and the overarching political system was not sufficient, and ended up being detrimental in the long run.

In the second revolutionary upheaval (1960s and 1970s), abolitionist forces made serious advances. The Black Panther Party had a tremendous political infrastructure, and like-minded groups like the Young Lords, the American Indian Movement, and the Weather Underground gained experience and coordinated effectively. Their political intentions were clear and well-articulated, and they managed to gain popular momentum. The formation of the Black Liberation Army marked a clear turning point in the revolutionary movement in the US. This was the most efficient guerrilla resistance in the US in the 20th century. But, as noted earlier, the BPP and BLA did not adequately coordinate. Russell Maroon Shoatz writes, "The same mistake that the civil rights movement had made was revisited upon the

BPP: Both had put too much stock in one facet of the resistance. With the civil rights movement there was too much focus on political work and not nearly enough on military components, and with the guerrilla group it was just the opposite."[3] For this struggle to have progressed it would have required greater coordination and a broader array of activities; solely focusing on one aspect of resistance is inherently inimical to political growth. For the abolitionist movement to expand in both depth and numbers we must encourage different organizing models to function cooperatively with precise political motivations, while also charting a militant strategy.

First, the revolutionary movement must vigorously direct its activities towards slavery/prison abolition and the abolition of all forms of captivity. The war against these institutions and their larger political appendages cannot be viewed as distinct struggles from the larger revolutionary conflict. These are the core stabilizing institutions for the entire state system; this is where the mechanisms of capitalism, slavery, anti-blackness, and the ever-expanding carceral system are created. The slave/prison relation has remained intact and its barbarism is now being unleashed on the entire populace.

It is telling that 46% of the federal prison population, almost half, is for drug offenses, essentially the underground economy of those excluded from economic opportunities. The second highest prison population, 16%, is for weapons charges: the criminalization of those trying to regain a measure of self-defense.

Yet one cannot calculate the pain so many families are forced to endure simply because of their social position. This cannot and will not be allowed to continue. In order to destroy this social relation, we have to abolish the prisons, the ICE facilities, the detention centers, and the American plantation as a whole.

Second, our longterm vision must be to abolish the State itself. It is clear that the nation-state, and the capitalist economy it upholds, make continued suppression inevitable. It removes people from political participation, and institutes control through institutionalized racism, patriarchy, and domination, turning life or death decisions over to a powerful minority. This violent apparatus is maintained by the entire judicial system, civic legislation and its threat of incarceration. Meanwhile, the State's relationship with capitalism keeps people in a constant state of pliability, as the resources they need to live are withheld.

The overarching scope of our struggle must focus on building abolitionist counter-power and helping people escape the plantation. While we fight to abolish prisons and the state structure, we must unequivocally fight alongside those who are now the target of state violence, with the intent of ending the entirety of this heinous system.

The basic focus of our struggle:

- The Abolitionist struggle must take up the immediate fight to abolish prisons, courts, and ICE detention facilities.

- As Abolitionists, we must fight unequivocally with Black, Latino, Native, Muslim people, and all those subjected to prison society and white supremacy.

- This struggle must be feminist, and predicated on queer and trans liberation.

- The Abolitionist struggle must fight for decentralized, commune-based political organization, and stand resolutely against capitalism and the State.

- The struggle must be oriented toward militant self-defense, and devise specific plans for offensive actions against reactionary forces.

- The Abolitionist long-term goal is to get rid of the justice system, the nation-state, and the capitalist economy.

These points should be the basic focus of our struggle, and in their light, we can then consider short-term and longer-term objectives in building a lasting, abolitionist revolutionary current, with a revolutionary purview to create a society without the State.

Short Term:
Establishing the Underground Railroad

The process of escape and defense is an immediate imperative with strategic and ethical implications. Communities are being targeted with mass incarceration, ethnic cleansing, and deportation with the goal of creating a racially homogenous, white supremacist society.

The slave/prison complex is the foundation of the oppressive apparatuses from the plantation, to the prison, to Immigration and Customs Enforcement (ICE) facilities. Our first objective must be to liberate people from these complexes. People already flee captivity, but we ourselves have the capacity to get people out of the hands of the State. Whether people are in incarceration, detention, deportation, or subject to white supremacist/patriarchal violence we must create the networks for them to escape and live with dignity. It is our duty to bring this process to a halt, as soon as possible, by any means necessary.

We are calling on all militants who take up this call to actively assist people in this way. An action as small as bailing someone out of jail, halting an ICE raid, or hiding somebody who refuses to return to parole has a profound effect on a person's life. For a more involved engagement, helping establish a network of safe houses, or establishing a neighborhood defense group against hate attacks or ICE incursions, can help contribute to a larger and more readily defensible underground railroad.

Potential immediate actions:

- Provide materials and resources for those fleeing captivity.
- Aid people crossing the border.
- Help establish a network of safe houses.
- Dismantle infrastructure used for an oppressive purpose.
- Make a bail fund.

- Set up a Rapid Response group of neighbors to stop ICE detentions.

- Help train Neighborhood Defense Units against hate attacks and police violence.

These are only a few of many possible interventions; the tactics are secondary to the outcome and certainly vary depending on location and resources. Generally, the abolitionist movement must do what it can to protect people who are hiding from the State, and to make it as difficult as possible for the State to continue its onslaught.

It is through this process that we must make self-defense and offensive action a focal point of our organizing.

For these actions to be successful, they must be organized entirely outside State apparatuses, and according to strict security measures. Due to this necessity, the networks and groups that arise from these activities, carry with them revolutionary potential. First, the underground railroad necessitates revolutionary defense. For example, people hiding immigrants in safe houses need protection from bigots and ICE. Secondly, offensive action becomes a focal point for organizing. If the State machinery can be halted first, then it cannot be used for its intended purpose. Finally, these projects are based on neighbors helping neighbors, not for any compensation, but for all the same reasons that create a strong community of resistance.

We first must make sure people can escape draconian institutions and then build towards autonomy with them so that they can continue to live outside reactionary State power. As people escape bondage we can begin to lay the foundations for a revolutionary project that can create an insuppressible counter-power.

Long Term:
Network of Abolitionist Councils

It is important to remember that our support will fail if it doesn't prove effective. The long term project for the abolitionist movement must be to create a new political reality and establish infrastructure that can render the State and capitalist institutions obsolete. We must build the capacity to defend our gains while we defeat our opponents. If we can focus our struggle on defeating slavery, detention, and fascist organizing, then the underground railroad will build resolute militant networks to combat the State. By fighting for those in captivity we can gradually integrate larger, more diverse groups into our councils.

The first steps toward building a larger network are already in existence. Networks of social centers, squats, and militants already exist and are politically active. They have an important role to play by bringing in new people, providing infrastructure for organizing, and creating a political narrative for the local and larger public. This growth creates new groups and networks that can provide resources for those who have escaped and those who are in struggle.

As we liberate people from detention, we are simultaneously building networks outside the State, and creating new relationships based on solidarity. Essentially the qualities that allow for the underground railroad to flourish, are the same ones that create a strong revolutionary movement. The underground railroad is the beginning-network that becomes the councils, self-defense units, and conflict resolution bodies of the future.

Building the infrastructure of the future:

* Neighborhood defense units or anti-fascist squads train others, helping bolster a network of locally based self-defense units.

* Revolutionary groups or social centers organize neighborhood councils.

* Connections born from the underground railroad strengthen the relationship between councils.

Through this process we can escape some of the problems of the previous abolitionist and 20th century vanguardist movements. Instead of subordinating the collectives to authoritarian leadership, or focusing on the seizure of the State, the communes and centers – immersed in their local struggle – become the political bodies of revolutionary organization. These bodies can coordinate nationally to respond to challenges from the State, and share resources and strategies as necessary.

If we can free people from bondage, organize new political bodies, and prepare to defend our liberated communities, we can proudly take our place in the continuity of the Abolitionist struggle, from The Great Dismal Swamp to Harpers Ferry to Wounded Knee or to the liberation of Assata Shakur.

Operating Principles

We intend for these operating principles to emphasize that we are building a revolutionary movement and take the wellbeing of participants the movement seriously.

- Express solidarity with all oppressed peoples.

- Support other revolutionary anti-state political organizations.

- Encourage a diversity of tactics utilizing direct action and mutual aid.

- Support our fighters.

    - Support political prisoners.

    - Aid militants who get injured or have legal troubles as a result of their revolutionary work.

- Non-collaboration: prohibit work with law enforcement, non-profit organizations, or government administration.

- Security.

    - Maintain personal anonymity unless collectively decided otherwise.

    - Be wary of journalists, and generally prohibit their presence.

    - Safeguard information about other revolutionaries.

    - Keep disagreements out of public forums.

Good security measures are necessary given the scope of our struggle. However beyond the obvious structural reasons, consistent security practices helps foster a culture of trust. The more people trust those around them, the more risks they are able to collectively take, allowing the movement to progress.

Similarly, supporting imprisoned revolutionaries is not only our duty, but sends the message to new participants: we will stand behind you for the long haul.

In this vein, we show respect for other revolutionary groups and individuals by keeping disagreements private. There are many tactics and discourses used by different groups, and even if we find one path more applicable than another, it would be foolish for us to tell another group that what they are doing is incorrect. In other words, we don't use criticism as a way to discredit other anti-authoritarian organizations. Such a practice only serves to demoralize potential collaborators and make the movement appear fractured and incapable in the eyes of the public. If we have criticism of certain approaches we only use it for our internal conversations: debating the benefits and potential pitfalls as we consider the next pragmatic steps we intend to take.

The success of the abolitionist movement depends on building a new political framework. By using direct action, that is, recuperating resources and destroying oppressive structures, communities in resistance begin enacting the very relationships and direct processes they intend to establish over the long run. The same goes for mutual aid. Neighbors and revolutionaries helping each other out with no other motivation than building a strong community is the ideal basis for the future of the resistance movement.

To create a community completely outside the overreaching arms of the State, it is imperative that we take a non-collaborationist stance with the State and all of its minions who seek to dampen our momentum, either by brute force, co-optation, or intimidation. This includes law enforcement, nonprofit organizations, and government agencies. Our job is to dismantle them and the disgraceful system they uphold, while putting in place these principles in order to strengthen the relationships between people within the movement.

Towards a Revolutionary Future

In the US today political institutions are incredibly unpopular, and the major institutions that make up the political framework of the country—the Congress, the Supreme Court, the Executive branch, and the media—are all increasingly viewed as illegitimate. As we race towards an abrupt shift in the global order, hastened by economic instability, environmental catastrophe, and racial strife, the US populace has become extraordinarily polarized. This is what led to the elevation of explicit white nationalists into the executive office.

While the US races into a state of decline, it is now positioned in its traditional role as the vanguard of international white supremacy and authoritarianism. Far right groups are gaining in prominence, the government is actively attempting to ethnically cleanse large segments of the population, and the veneer of liberal legitimacy is now gone. With this state of flux and violence, the marginalized and criminalized desperately need a real political solution, and the support of people who will take an uncompromising stand. We must be ready to act in the opening created by the government's own self-destruction.

As anti-authoritarians, we are poised at the front of the pivotal struggle of humanity: our world will either continue its descent towards the right and its desire for oppression, genocide, and intolerance, or we will organize for liberation, leaving behind any traces of hierarchy and domination. Our goal is to orient the struggle, to renew a widespread commitment towards revolutionary abolitionism and to reemerge from the sidelines of history. The prison and the detention center are merely the physical manifestations of the all-encompassing captivity the State seeks to force upon us. We must re-establish the underground railroad to liberate criminalized people from captivity. If constructed mindfully, this track, rather than lead to temporary refuge or perpetual hiding, has the potential to finally bring the plantation system to an end.

We have crafted this document as a call to all revolutionaries. To everyone who is oppressed, to all those striving to live with dignity, to the brave ones fighting in the struggle for liberation, and to those who have no choice but to fight every day: we ask for you to fight alongside us and struggle with us toward liberation.

A new paradigm for revolution has been established, to be taken up by dedicated revolutionaries, autonomous territories, guerrillas in armed struggle, and all those engaged in the global drive towards liberation and away from statehood, capitalism, patriarchy, and domination. Collective societies, from the maroons to Rojava, have fostered insurrectionary situations that build, from the inside out, indestructible communities.

The success of such communities, from their duration to their territorial gains and continued autonomy, has set a standard we can strive towards.

Those who fought for liberation here in the US have left an important legacy. As we dig the trenches of our struggle, we draw from the lessons of this past, and proudly carry on the struggle in the memory of our fighters. It is their sacrifices that will propel us to the next stage of the struggle, and the resurgence of their fortitude and bravery that invigorates our commitments. We promise to all those who have previously risked everything for liberation, who have lived and died under the oppressive yoke of this country, and all those still struggling for a better life, that we will put all our strength towards building communities so powerful that they will repel any attempt, from within or without, to reestablish the oppressive power of white supremacy, patriarchy, the State and capital.

We will burn down the American plantation once and for all.

Works Cited

1. Wilderson III, Frank B. "The Prison Slave as Hegemony's (Silent) Scandal, Social Justice , Vol. 30, No. 2 (92), (2003), p. 22.

2. Umoja, Akinyele Omowale. Repression Breeds Resistance: The Black Liberation Army and the Radical Legacy of the Black Panther Party. New Political Science 21.2 (1999), 131-154.

3. Shoatz, Russell Maroon. Maroon The Implacable. PM Press, (2013), p. 97.

4. Davis, Angela. Freedom Is a Constant Struggle: Ferguson, Palestine, and the Foundations of a Movement. Haymarket Books, (2016), p. 71.

5. Wilderson III, Frank B. "The Prison Slave as Hegemony's (Silent) Scandal, Social Justice , Vol. 30, No. 2 (92), (2003), p. 20.

6. The Committee of Diplomacy of Kongreya Star. "About the Work and Ideas of Kongreya Star, the Women's Movement in Rojava. (2016).

7. Biehl, Janet. Rojava's Communes and Councils, http://www.biehlonbookchin.com/rojavas-communes-and-councils/ (2015).

8. Ramírez, Gloria Muñoz. Chiapas: Portrait of the Resistance, http://countervortex.org/node/6766. (2009).

9. Shirley, Neal and Saralee Stafford. Dixie Be Damned: 300 Years of Insurrection in the American South. AK Press, (2015).

10. Bonanno, Alfredo M. And We Will Still Be Ready To Storm The Heavens Another Time: Against Amnesty, http://theanarchistlibrary.org/library/alfredo-m-bonanno-andwe-will-still-be-ready-to-storm-the-heavens-another-timeagainst-amnesty, (1984).

11. Experiences in Rojava: Interview with an Anarchist YPG Volunteer, http://kurdishquestion.com/article/3865-experiences-in-rojava-interview-with-an-anarchist-ypgvolunteer. (2017).

12. Ayboğa, Ercan. Consensus is Key: New Justice System in Rojava, http://new-compass.net/articles/consensus-keynew-justice-system-rojava. (2014).

13. TATORT Kurdistan. Democratic Autonomy in North Kurdistan. New Compass, (2013).

14. Hartman, Saidiya. Scenes of Subjection: Terror, Slavery, and Self-Making in Nineteenth-Century America, (1997) p.100.

15. Zinn, Howard. "Slavery Without Submission, Emancipation Without Freedom." A People's History of the United States. http://www.historyisaweapon.com/defcon1/zinnslaem10.html.

16. Shakur, Assata. "Women in Prison: How It Is With Us." History is a Weapon, (1978).

17. Aileen. Mujeres Libres, http://flag.blackened.net/revolt/talks/mujeres.html. (1995).

18. Dirik, Dilar.Yazidi Women: From Genocide to Resistance, http://kurdishquestion.com/oldarticle.php?aid=yazidiwomen-from-genocide-to-resistance. (2016).

19. Gupta, Rahlia. Women's Co-operatives in Rojava, https://cooperativeeconomy.info/womens-co-operatives-in-rojava/. (2016).

Made in the USA
San Bernardino, CA
21 June 2020

73984011R00055